ALSO BY JOAN CAROLE HAND

Poetry

East of July (Cross Cultural Communications, 2004)
Entrances to Nowhere (Cross Cultural Communications, 1977)
The Facts of Life (Cross Cultural Communications, 1987)

Novella
Your Witch (Despa Press, 1971)

MOMMY

AND OTHER POEMS

poems by

Joan Carole Hand

Finishing Line Press
Georgetown, Kentucky

MOMMY

AND OTHER POEMS

ACKNOWLEDGMENTS

Acknowledgment and thanks are due to the editors and publishers of
the following anthologies and magazines, wherein the poems noted first
appeared, *Paumanok Interwoven* in 2013 ("Blue Hydrangeas"), and *Korean
Expatriate literature*, Issue #23 in 2019 ("The Boat"), and *Bridging the
Waters*, Vol. III in 2020 ("A Slice of Life"). Thanks Andrea Katz for her
invaluable computer assistance and to Cross Cultural Communications for
their ongoing poetic support over the past 40 years. Special thanks also go to
my daughter Emily Axelrod, who has been a constant help throughout this
creative process, and to my son Daniel Axelrod, who has been my eyes and
my ears in the compilation of this manuscript – an invaluable assistant in
helping to bring every image to life.

Publisher: Leah Huete de Maines
Editor: Christen Kincaid
Cover Art: Photo of Betty Hand and J.C. Hand, taken in the Catskills,
        1963, courtesy of J.C. Hand
Author Photo: Daniel Axelrod

Cover Design: Erik Gliedman, Erik Christian Photography

Order online: www.finishinglinepress.com
        also available on amazon.com

Author inquiries and mail orders:
Finishing Line Press
P. O. Box 1626
Georgetown, Kentucky 40324
U. S. A.

Table of Contents

Blue Hydrangeas...1

Mommy 3

Queen Esther..6

A Certain Someone 8

The Boy in the Sharp Blue Shirt 9

A Scalding Whiteness 10

An Appalachian Spring...11

A Slice of Life 12

A Portrait in Two Parts...14

The Boat..16

A Summer Offering...17

A Statement of Loss..19

Escape 23

On the Outside 24

House 25

With All Due Respect 27

Ode to the Computer..29

Still Dancing...30

Keeping me Safe..32

Defying Time 33

For my grandchildren,
Zoe Samantha,
Katrina Francis
and Dustin Harold

ABOUT THE AUTHOR

Joan Carole Hand was born in Brooklyn, N.Y. in 1943. She migrated east on Long Island to Rocky Point in 1969. Trained as a fiction writer, she also found her poetic voice with her first book, *Entrances to Nowhere* (Cross-Cultural Communications, 1977), followed by *The Facts of Life* (Cross-Cultural Communications, 1987), and East of July (Cross-Cultural Communications, 2004). Her poetry has been published in literary quarterlies and magazines throughout the United States and internationally, including in Sicily, Wales and South Korea. In *Mommy*, she has brought together all of her sense memories, all the nuances of light, shadow, and color, and the lives of the people, who she encountered during her more than fifty years of swimming to the rhythm of the waves. She holds an A.B. from Bard College, an M.A. from the Johns Hopkins University Writing Seminars, and an M.F.A. from the University of Iowa Writers' Workshops. She is a mother of three, a grandmother of three and a cat mother of one.

Blue Hydrangeas

The other woman finds time to manicure her nails.
The other woman is perfect where her rival fails?
  – Nina Simone

There is a time of blue hydrangeas, when the hot,
blunt August sun bullies my heart into leaving
you, my lover boy – you and that other woman.

Sometimes, I think of you with her, and knowing
you as I do, your love life could, indeed, be true,
because you have always existed on the ball of
the moment, with the gusto of a body surfer.

The ocean blue-black, bereft of ice, and the
ocean, like movable glass, covered with the
crushed silvery tips of waves, disappearing, and
appearing with a forcefulness reminiscent of sex.

Of course, your other woman is no substitute for
me. I imagine the wedge of her bottle-rinsed hair,
too yellow to be evocative, like a tuneless flute
mounting the sky. HER FLUTE, NOT MINE!

I see the two of you waiting on that wraparound
deck, beneath a lilac sky – despite her wanton,
milkless breasts – still watching the boats in
Huntington Harbor heading out to sea.

Of course, you see, the other woman is not a
substitute for me. I picture you both in clown
suits, and I watch in a jealous haze, as the suits
fall off. The sun is shining down in all its glory,
so I can make out the roots of her painted hair.

And so, my lover boy, I've known you since
we were both nineteen, your eyes back then,
the color of new hydrangeas, like a patch of
rain loose in the autumn sky. We lay side by
side, on that hard, grey mattress in my dorm,
back in the early '60s, when such things were
not *de rigueur*.

Do you remember, lover boy, my breasts were
like brown pears, and my shoulders were wide
and determined as a shelf holding up a wall.
My hair, you see, was gold, and auburn, and
honey brown (but did you appreciate it?), so
soft in that bright autumn breeze, the air lifting
us up and farther up into the stratosphere,
enabling us to flee like astronauts into a
weightless world.

And I tell you, lover boy, I am the other woman ...
insane with color, and I bleed remembering her
antics. It is as if the distance can be ascended ...
for I am the distance now, and I am the space
between the moments.

September 2007

Mommy

Mommy, are you dreaming?
Shifting , backward through time –
like a baby on a swing?
Mommy, are you swinging –
somewhere beyond the whiteness
of your endless flight?
To a place from which you only disappear –
like …
the fly-a-way lightness of ash.

***

Mommy, I bought you a bouquet
of paper flowers – invisible,
like you are now.
Still …
I dipped them in paint,
the white for death,
and the gold aflame with fall.

***

And Mommy,
I set them in
a large glass jar – a vase almost
"Beth Shalom Chapels Inc."
and yes …
with a blue Star of David
etched into the front of it,
not letting me
forget that, once, gray wax
had imprinted its tired flame,
staining the parameters of a window
that doesn't exist,
the flame lasting
for over a week.

***

Mommy, you are paper now –
as in papier-mâché,
your face suddenly shielded
by a cold, and wet exterior.
Because … now, once more,
you are a handful of identical ashes
– blackened and burnt …
But if I look long enough, Mommy …
your face is also the face of
a puppet's –
hardened, pointy, old.

***

Mommy, I celebrate
the blackness of your own mother's eyes –
those eyes, so forlorn,
they are disappearing into the light,
as I wait by the water
for the brightness to return to yours.

***

Mommy, you are
pasted to the sky
and …
you are *not*
my Mommy anymore.
In fact, I am my own *mommy* now.
And still, I repent
because you are silver,
silver or perhaps,
white-gold.
I wear you like a locket
with your picture sewn inside.

And yes, I continue to repent
because …
you were my sidekick,
my partner forever,
my best friend.

***

Together,
we penetrated
the highest of the high tides,
swimming against every current,
and testing
the invisibility of the fishes
that we kept failing and failing to catch.
And that's when you warned me, Mommy.
So *please*
tell me once again …
how I must conceal my heart
from my enemies
and guard the roots
of every long-lost smile.

February 20, 2007

Queen Esther

For my granddaughter, Zoe Samantha Robinson

Zoe, you are Queen Esther, first-place
winner of that most significant ancient
beauty pageant that your cousin Mordecai
brought you to at the palace of King
Ahasuerus – King of the Persian Empire
in Shushan – who, after he'd thrown
his then-faithless wife Vashti to the dogs,
selected you.

Esther, to be his queen; you, the most
beautiful maiden in all of Shushan by
the light of the almost-April sky. It was the
month of ancient Adar, and, there, quelling
your thirst for spring, fresh apricots sewn into
the centers of three-cornered Hamentashen,
your lips proceed to conquer the thirst of
sunlight and yellow daffodils, proceeding
to lean forward over the black, succulent
earth after you managed to have the evil
Prime Minister Hamen hung for setting
out to murder all the Jews in ancient Persia.

You, Zoe-Esther, queen of all the Persian
Jews; you, striding across old Babylonian
roads – made not of asphalt (not yet of course)
but of a searingly strong stone – to take you
anywhere you wanted to go. You, your hair
the color of Cypress leaves, tinged with sunlight.
You, beside the Caspian Sea or Black Sea;
there, the fishes are thirsting for you to mount
their very tips, and hurl your achingly wild
spring torso into a wilderness of ocean.

They, thirsting for you to control their
very essence, enabling you to swim backwards
to Adar, to the March-April time, and a place
where you made Purim happen. You, with
the wild strokes of a dancer, taking you
both backwards to somewhere so familiar.
Zoe-Esther, the conqueror, if that King
hadn't fallen at your feet, your greatness
in Biblical time would continue to repeat
in a golden flash of memory
concealing nothing.

The past is telling us about time, never
stopping those miniature blossoms that
slip like silver fish beneath the depth and
breath of oceans that can never quite be
concealed …

And yes, like the original Esther –
your own mother's middle name
and the name of your great-great
grandmother, born in the blue-black
region of a Russian *shtetl*, your
achingly, alluring young self –
princess and queen in one.
You're a beacon toward the future,
lighting up a past that these biblical
moments will never ever let us forget.

April 9, 2016

A Certain Someone

For my granddaughter, Katrina Francis Robinson

Born one day after the ides of March,
with a perfectly formed pink head,
but with a scalp so wonderfully orange
that would bloom soon enough into
circles of soft redness – a signal of
the girl, the shy but fierce little actress
who would become, so easily, Annie,
in *Annie*, or Cinderella, striding
raggedly into the woods in *Into the Woods,*
or Nala in *The Lion King*, with one
crisscross braid down your supple back.

Katrina, who was Cubby, one of the Lost Boys
in *Peter Pan.* And, finally, you were Fantine
in *Les Misérables*, a dress the blue of dawn
with sleeves all puffy and white, and a stiff velvet
ribbon, crisscrossing around your elegant waist,
to hold you altogether. And your eyes are
blooming with melody, so the stage lets
loose its invisible moorings just in recognition
of your smile.

March 23, 2017

The Boy in the Sharp Blue Shirt

For my grandson, Dustin Harold Hartwick

Dustin climbs trees, his thick-soled
sneakers catching hold, each branch
as ladder-like as fresh rope. And Dustin,
who is eight, reads his volume of *Stuart
Little* by E.B White, carefully
in a reclineable living room chair, tilting
it this way and that, eyes on the prize of
each word that commits a particular image
to memory.

While Stuart Little, the mouse, has spectacles that
are perfect for him to peruse each word, his
face pursed in a smile that tells just how
much he knows: A thing or two, just like
Dustin – in fact Dustin has his very own
mouse living in a cozy glass tank, in a
bright, square house in Parsippany, N.J.

And in that picture that his Granny took
of him, that mouse, named Princess, is
retiring onto his neck and then suddenly
makes a mad dash for his shoulder
 – landing there. My only grandson
is wearing a sharp blue shirt, with
his dreamy eyes, his every-which-way
brown hair, which gleams through
the camera's lens.

His hair, with a proud remembrance of
the blonde from his babyhood years, still
gleams. His room is full of wood cabinets.
On one shelf: his tiny laptop and, of course,
his Batman alarm clock. He is now holding
that mouse to his heart. His half-open lips
preparing for a song.

August 15, 2018

A Scalding Whiteness

For my cousins, Alyson and Loren

Myra, you left without saying goodbye. You, shorn
of the memory of anyone at all. Your sight, bereft
of my eyes – the eyes of your favorite cousin,
for we were almost blood sisters. And who could
imagine your daughters – true sisters, whom you kind of
left to me – to accommodate our memories,
to evoke the specters of who we were, as if you
would have to exist through them and would
forever.

You left without saying goodbye. And yet back
on that fire escape in Crown Heights, you
and I were an item, your freckled nose pointed
perkily into the air; your shiny, black hair, so straight
and, most significantly, your eyes, commandeering
all who knew us to *stay, stay, stay* as you were,
as we were. And when we cavorted on the sand in
Riis Park, in our sharp, clingy bathing suits – it was all
to attract the boys who passed us by! The air, filled
with ocean smells and sunscreen. It was a pineapple
balminess, as side by side we swam, and broke the rhythm
of our strokes, discussing life itself. But I want you
to know how wonderful your girls are – with me still.
Their lovely eyes, different than yours with perhaps
a deeper brightness. But with a tossing of their heads
I see you (the two of us), back in our time.

You left without saying a proper goodbye. So
I am constantly conjuring up an image of your
keen, familiar face. Because I too am just beyond
that not so subtle divide, my mind, almost an
unfamiliar place. Still with an unforgiving
patience, I wait for time to finally transmute
an irrevocable darkness into a scalding whiteness.
For you Myra. For your lost, unfinished life …

April 26, 2018

An Appalachian Spring

Regarding the music of Aaron Copeland

Wanda, Wanda, Wanda, with the curling hair in a Marilyn
Monroe cut. And like Marilyn, you are wearing lipstick –
a cherry-red saturated with orange, coral and peach – a
reflection of a song of butterflies. They are soaring beyond
the ocean's bubbling space – soaring beyond the trees in spring,
before they will fill in those segments of light still familiar from
last winter.

Wanda, Wanda, you are here in your sandy-colored shoes, and gold
heart-shaped bracelets, and necklaces, and glowing hoop earrings.
And now, here in the present, you will let time, like butter, slide
beyond your fingers. And you will lift the May daffodils as you
plant marigolds, geraniums, tulips, sunflowers. The air is replete
with your yellowness.

May 19, 2018

A Slice of Life

For Wanda

Someday, deep in July, the air
saturated with heat – a whiteness
clings to our skin like laughter –
we glance at each other's lips
and realize how much a pair
we are – me, with my Earth-brown
short shorts, my hair, with an
over-coating of auburn, flung
loosely up and yours close-cropped
shouting its blondness into the
distance that we share, like a
latter-day Lucy and Ethel.

Full of mischief and guile,
we float along, one aisle
and another of Aldi,
shopping for mini-circles
of Brooklyn salami packaged
in plastic tight as mini girdles.

Brie, full of a tart softness, and
New England sharp cheddar
(blocks of it) and finally high
on a shelf Choceur (smooth & creamy)
Swiss chocolate – thick bars of
raisin and nut not so much
sweet as invading our gut
with a quality to die for!

Finally, we slide into the
air-conditioned bliss of
your car – you call it a
Bentley, but it's really a Lexus,
with its motor quick to abbreviate
the distance between earth and sky.
We fly …

September 8, 2018

A Portrait in Two Parts

For my daughter, Jessica Robinson

<u>Part one</u>

First-born,
with your eyes that
would have been chocolate
like my own, but instead, though
still doe-shaped were the green
of a tropical sea – a chartreuse color,
yet almost gold like fish – the shade
that snorkelers see watching and
waiting for schools of them to pass.
But, still, if those fish scurry
too deep their colors can reflect
the glint of a silver shark's skin.

Part two

But in that picture that you
painted of yourself, you were
just sixteen, piercing your ears with
tiny silver bell-shaped earrings,
the light reaching down
your sharp chin. So, Jessica, my
first-born, with eyes so wide and
beautiful, your cupid-bow mouth,
so curvaceous, as if awaiting – with
a passion I have to call intense – for
that haunting suggestion of approval
you always craved.

So how could I
not love you back then, your hair a
deep cherry yet at the same time
almost auburn, then a kind of purple,
and even in some way blonde, really
more yellow-orange, wild stretches of
color that stand you in good stead.
Your forehead wide, a combination
of every shade of the rainbow from
pinkish beige to an almost vacuous
stark white. And those eyes, so
bright, they stare out of that canvas
at me, your only mother still lost in
those vast and almost happy spaces
on your face – the only ones
you now at long last relent
to give me back.

September 25, 2017

The Boat

For Roy, on the occasion of his 79th birthday

Root for yourself love – for there is
no one more deserving than you! And
if age be but a figment of a motion – so
be it, we will not conquer the distance
between mortality and time. We will
ride time itself, as if a boat flowing
secretly along the wild and swelling
sea. For we are all in the same boat,
baby! But with an indomitable courage,
we can tear down the "No Exit" sign
that hangs voicelessly from the bow.
And we will make certain the
gendarmes can't catch us. For
bereft of anything solidly reminding
us of our old home, we will allow
time to help us tread along together,
before we make that long, invisible
swim back to where we started from,
the self, recognizing the flash of a
dream – happening too many eons
ago to count …

July 12, 2018

A Summer Offering

For Jessica and Andrew Delligatti

Jessica Ann, I see you see …
as in circa *Roman Holiday,*
your long and dappled hair,
a blondness mingling
with a coffee brown. You
wrap it over and over
on top of your head –
a sleek, but comfortable
hairdo. You are a modern
day Audrey Hepburn keening
for her Gregory Peck, who
exists this modern day as
Andrew Delligatti.

You are his princess, she who
has escaped the restraints
of life cooped up in a city
pace – somewhere lost in the
distance of a world you
sometimes like to forget.
And you can be both shy
in the shadows of those
Roman arches, but with
a spirit that knows no
bounds …

You shine, the girl, who,
through the window of her
newly wood-shingled house
in Rocky Point, can just
make out that one high rock
lapped by the blue-grey
waters of Long Island Sound –
a small but substantial rock
surfacing with a theatricality

that knows no bounds – only
revealing itself between
tides …

It is your anchor and your
strength, a guideline of
steadiness defining you
as you move across the
ultra-green lawn with
your three cats – Minnie,
Sammy, Lucy – past those
pink and yellow porch flowers,
into a reverent kind of distance,
at your enduring seashore holiday.
Here, two celebrate their home.

July 2, 2019

A Statement of Loss

For my brother, Frederic Warren Hand

You, my brother, were an only child,
lost on the streets and avenues
we called Brooklyn, in a time
impossible to forget.

You, my brother, were an only child –
are, were, still are born of an empathy
that your music, then and now, has
always managed to convey. You,
my only brother, though you are
not born of my time, your body
reaching out beyond those
woodframed windows in a tenement
(though fancier than that). Are you
hearing me now?

The swish and creak of tires on
those hard, exhausted streets
with the motion of old cars:
Ford Fairlanes and Plymouth
Belvederes, and, eventually Dodge
Darts, darting out every which way,
along the boulevards we still
remember in a time when music
moved inside you – within a motion
made by your baby fingers, poised
between those up and down sensations.

It is a syncopation of sight and a
tenderness lost to time – your fingers softening
the brutal dusk of your tiny life, and
of your then-tiny life, and now becoming
you here, first here then further off,
into somewhere to a place at first
you did not understand – at least not

with your mind per se – that suffocatingly
large, dark rhythm you march beside
along those endless streets. The trees
above you are maples, sycamores, oaks
their branches soughing and singing in
the lost spring wind.

Then they are reaching, no, leaping
up above the black asphalt, their colors
taking you down through Crown Heights,
in a time when music moved inside of you,
with a motion made by your fingers at
first, just those baby fingers. They
are softening the brutal dusk of your
tiny life and becoming you, here, then
further off into somewhere, to a place
at first you did not understand.

You, my brother, were an only child. You
can tell from those almost ancient photos
of you – almost in sepia, though, practically
speaking, you could see the lines and shadows,
an infinitesimal nuance of grey and grief.
You are in your striped polo shirt and high-topped
sneakers and little dungarees folded up at just
below the knee – with a baseball cap that if in
color would have been blue. And you are strumming
your first guitar, the branches above you dancing
in the wind. Their sounds are like colors taking
you through all of Brooklyn, your father at the
helm – with a beat-up kind of growl lodged in
his almost ancient throat.

He is still a fifty-year-old man. He is barely
working and your mother in a striped shirt-waist
dress, her hair a cap of endless curls …
Your mommy – where was she then?

You her only son? Did she see the chimes in
your eyes and the every which way your brave
brown eyes reflected so much night
and you alone, somewhere, somehow music round
your heart – you played for her. But it was not with
your musical psyche alone, but with your soul
(what was the beginning, and what was left
of it now), since you've given up so many pieces
presently made up of it.

It was like the basketballs you loved, and the
tinkling bright ping pong balls, and the round
circles of wood that you played Nok-Hockey with.
So where are you going now, during those moments
when the sound of your first guitar retells the dance
of spring leaves above your head and the motionless
agenda of the *tsuris* of other people's
lives … So, I see you defying the rising and the
sinking of Bach's Brandenburg Concerto, a dance
not so much a complement of time but a recognition
of the way even the air you take for granted now is laced
with empathy. It is an empathy your music conveys
so automatically, and, you, presently with a passion
perhaps you no longer know, in a way that you
have forgotten me.

Though I am your only sibling –
strolling along that exercise track
we call life – me your only sister
beneath the pitter-pat of rain
pinpointing the powerless earth – the
wild and spotted, the most resilient
earth, resting now. I am swimming
through Crown Heights, an ocean of
motion now suddenly exhausted enough
to settle down on one hardwood bench.
It is cemented to the cobbled earth on

Eastern Parkway. So, finally now, you
are completely lost to me beyond
the little, iron-gated entrance to the garden on
Carroll Street – so loomingly large now
at night. And below me, is our four-story
apartment building; and you are maybe, just
maybe, still managing to sing to me, even
though I am no longer there.

October 2017

Escape

For Ruth, who herself becomes a camera whenever she
locates the yolk of a sunflower on the lens of each sensitive eye

You are your own Oma, now with streaks of sun-splashed
brightness adding to the blonde in your hair. Still, back then
in 1950, there was the train screeching along from East to West
Germany. Tipping. Tippling. Better sit up straight or the VoPo
will catch you. Russkie Polizei in khaki uniforms, tight.
And Sabrina, in soft pullovers and checkered wool skirts, with
high leather shoes. She is clutching her stuffed dog Stroofie
(some straw missing then and still to this day). Sabrina had
to choose, "One toy only," her sister Erika said. So, Petra the
puppe, with her painted head and open and shut glass eye
– goodbye. And now she must get rid of der mann before you
or he might figure you all out. "Schönes Mädchen," he said,
"So pretty," and you tried to wriggle away, to shoot him back
a smile. Scary. Suspicious. You wanted to say, that you're not
really a pumpkin with so many layers of thick clothing. You
were actually a fairy princess. And then he grinned with an eerie
kind of grimness and a large lachen, too. And Mama, sweating
across the aisle, pretending not to know them! Because that
was the law: only singles could leave the East. But the train
had stopped and now there is silence. So, you had fooled the
VoPo. Gott sei Dank! And finally, you could go on your way.
Sunlight sugaring the air. Last part of their journey. Is now,
by plane. And on the mountains below, a storybook green with
peaks of snow. Vanilla icing. And the wind is fingering the
distance between time past and time to come. Your
picture-postcard world, breaking apart. Frankfurt. Finally
descending. You are rushing by stucco houses, the color of
pulled taffy, etched with brown bric-a-brac. And the roofs are
red as licorice, though it all seems to be a cartoon. But with
real doll structures. You can grab onto yours suddenly lifting
it high above your head with one hand … because you are home!

April 27, 2018

On the Outside

For my father, Frank Hand

They said you left some pieces
of yourself in the old cellar.
Insignificant items, I quickly
assumed, within the bowels of
a place replete with memories.

They found a dented suitcase,
some shirts with collars, dust-rimmed,
their initial whiteness gone, along with
a pair of rusty cufflinks, and too many
wrinkled ties to count. So many visions
of you, alive, alive! While I so selfishly
remained on the outside …

October 18, 2018

House

For my children Jessica, Emily & Daniel

House, I love you, house. You are with me
always and you are substantially not. House,
with the windows facing south, east, west, and
north. Those windows – like square, gun-metal
eyes that encompass a view of that mobile
water – grey-blue with white tips, disappearing
whenever the currents decide to pick them up and
shake them into sometimes angry suds. Long Island
Sound, breathing and at the same time breathless;
once the sight of that water caused my own eyes
to blink in remembrance of my body – lithe and
wild and summer-browned, traversing the distance
between now and yesterday.

House, your innards will always be mine, though
I left you now so long ago. My upstairs blue bathroom,
almost pastel, with little square, white tiles below
a polished wood-encased sink. And the tub, a jacuzzi,
magenta almost, that rocks me forward and backward.

House, I still love you, always will. And in that
gold and white upstairs bedroom where I lay with
labor pains for my second child – as if I was the sea
itself, as I twisted and turned on what was once
my marital bed – it was a dance for you, house,
and, in you, that baby became both you (and me)
with her (later I saw it) strawberry-blonde head.

House, you are mine again suddenly invading
my essence – who I was, and me now, with my hair
bereft of the color it once was. House, it was here
in the wide and sun-shiny kitchen with its fierce
ceramic floor that I once boiled, broiled, baked
and fried for my family beside the strong cabinets –
wood shining.

And of course, there is the main-floor bathroom,
tiled the yellow of a legal pad from tip to toe,
with the stark, white, high tub,
its curved black iron legs, supporting us.

But, house, where is my downstairs study
facing the sea, with its apple-green rug?
The tall rectangular windows framed by
leaf-green drapes, and the homemade
floor-to-ceiling bookcase built into paneled
walls. And my old oak desk isn't there anymore,
to watch me in a dance of gathered thoughts –
running, now one into the other like a field of
windblown dandelions.

Still, house, my last vision of you is upstairs,
again facing the North. And we are wildly
calibrating the spread of raindrops, as they
pelt the windows with the tiny, lacy smears
of circles going nowhere. And I see you my
husband, as if from another time, with your rumpled
hair and black beard. And then I blot you out forever,
though it's not about the sex, or our windswept view
of the dark and churning ocean, but the fact that
all of a sudden, nothing can stop me from vacuuming
the hard, greyish, rust-colored carpet. And I am
here, myself alone beneath a vaulted A-shaped ceiling
before I hurry downstairs swapping my psyche for
a smooth, glass doorknob, which automatically
twists open, bringing me finally outside beyond
that old, though unchipped maple door.

January 15, 2018

With All Due Respect

You say that empathy
must be selectively
employed (illnesses vary
on certain occasions).
Well-chosen, perhaps,
though we do not know
by whom, as in by
which God? In that
case it is easy to
dismiss the shot of
terror fired from a gun,
negated not by time or
motion, nor the spark of
absolution one knows
another's *tsuris* will command.

In this case, the stranger
becomes the more superior
victim, standing a hundred
feet higher than oneself,
and higher than any other
victim has ever stood – her
otherness making her just
more saintly, though not
actually a real-life saint
just one more honorable,
less culpable for her fate.

You see that tragedy
compels empathy between
good friends, and, as it
were, strangers. Because
behind one's smile (after
the tragic truth has been
revealed), there is an
instantaneous "God Bless
you," and an automatic prayer

of safekeeping, a hope to
guard one's children and one's
self from this, a similar
pain.

So, understand
that first I want to say
 – there are differences
in people, as if each were
their own separate species,
some more legitimately at
risk than the rest of us.
For is a crazy person less
entitled to experience that
extra stab of terror that
comes from his or her
very own turf?

Not negating the risk
that mostly artists take
 – that automatic sense
of denial, seeded with
an old familiar apprehension
of an unknown world.
Because death consumes
life, in some sure-footed
style that only those
who stay alive
can begin to believe –
the terror lives behind
the laughter,
the kind consumed
by the rhythm of the
silent indiscriminate gods.

March 22, 2006

Ode to the Computer

First you see it, then you don't.
It truly is a disappearing act, without
reason or season on a screen, as some call
it (though erroneously). It is something,
actually invisible, a whole other
picture, from moment to moment, or
of a message, often, so sadly unretrieved,
or just a series of fine lines, a figment
of a thought manifesting itself as a
group of symbols pretending to be
words – concepts in the shape of a gift,
a group of symbols pretending to be
overwhelmingly alive to do what they
call texts – which are impinging
on the ball of each slippery finger's tip.
Dead. Without imbibing the odor of
paper, ink, the cursive motion of tangible
grammatical objects. They are the tiny,
smooth pitter-patter of lost fingers, though
not in a dance, nor a quick, wild slippery
fugue, but night tiptoeing as daylight – under
statements as if allowing for a false perspicacity,
a lingering feeling just fraught with overwhelming
quickness, the passage of breathing with the
numbness of a kind of eerie silence. And on
that laptop just particular keys that could instantly,
summarily die because all the power in the world
cannot keep those words from shutting down – with
neither an overwhelming or necessary notice – no,
there is no chance of any kind of resurrection, just
an eerie imminent death.

December 11, 2017

Still Dancing

*For Anna and John Stephens, on the occasion
of my birthday ... looking forward, looking back.*

I'm still dancing,
with the same
freewheeling
motion that
reminds me of
balloons lost in
the clouds, and my
pointed toes
traverse the
rim of a tight
rope and land
on the point
of a star ...

I'm still dancing,
and I'm fifteen, and
a girl spinning
into a yellow sky, with
my auburn hair
cascading downward
and flaring upward,
and swaying – my
whole body involved in
a solar system
belonging to me,
but only if I continue
to dance, though
it's not the same dance
because now I can
gauge a series
of moments sharp
enough to sense the substance
of my trip. That
height leads to higher

and higher heights,
and time and flight
are the keys to
going home.

So, I'm still dancing, and
continuing to race
as if my body had a will of
its own – because now
I'm mastering the royal
blue steps to the
sky ... the wild blue wind
lifting me up and into a
rarefied atmosphere.
Thus, I can conquer the
past as well as the future,
where I am one with my
balloons, and I am finally
in the *now* of it.

And a light that propels me
into conquering the past
belongs to me,
more and more,
while I'm still dancing,
alright. The light
is on, spraying and spraying
its slippery whiteness,
as I go leaping and climbing,
twirling and twisting,
and finally waking up –
ending up *on center stage.*

October 2008

Keeping Me Safe

How could I have known, my son,
how quickly I would realize that
your father's recently deceased third
wife and I, his first wife, would wear
the same size T-shirt: an extra-large?
Such an interesting coincidence! That
shirt spelled out M-O-M in white with
a backing of orange and blue. Perhaps
her favorite colors or maybe mine.
"I'm sorry," my son intoned, "But
you see she never wore it, and I nicked
off the little sales tag." So did that mean
his stepmother and I had so much in
common – both of us cast adrift, she by
death, but me by life – both of us
abandoned in a way? And I too live
by a beach. Mine is in the Northeast
with massive firs, white birches and
oaks surrounding the sea. Hers in a
southern state with endless, softer,
whiter sand bordered by a filigree of
extra-green palm trees. Luckily, I'm
still on a waiting list for the day when
I will come to her. And, in fact, I do
have one memory, though a vague
one or maybe not. Her face, her short,
straight hair, brownish with an overall
orangey tinge. She wore clear glasses
and sort of hugged me in that little
theater, waiting for my granddaughter's
starring performance in *Annie.*
Would I almost recognize her again,
especially if I wore the shirt
you bequeathed to me, and would I
become invisible too soon as well?
Or would it serve, for now, as mostly
a warning – a way of keeping me safe?

Defying Time

For Wini

Two cousins – five-feet tall,
give or take a half inch
(their mothers' height).
The younger, with tidy,
short, once-brunette
hair now stabbed with
pixels of gray and, here
and there, white; the older,
almost defying time, her
shoulder-length hair tinted a
reddish earth tone, as in clay.

Now both in
tight bathing caps, she
with a rubber-rimmed
mask – her supple breath,
thus contained, then released
at will; and I, the older, in
blue-rimmed goggles
adhering to the spaces
around my same dark eyes.

Together we head into Long
Island Sound with its extra-wide
'waterized' pleats – the
idea to slither between the
stitching. Magically within
the swells, we slip with heads
twisting in that cool and inky brew.
Splash after splash, we progress
toward Connecticut, the sun
yoking each neck, lightening
our faces; we are as if one, our
breaths defying time …

November 1, 2020

PRAISE FOR *MOMMY*

"In this impressive new collection, Joan Carole Hand offers her reader a deeply realized and convincing inventory of family and relationship, rooted in the rich soil of the poet's own life and aspirations. The speaker in these poems directly addresses specific individuals in Hand's life – principally but not exclusively family members – a subject she approaches with candor and directness of gaze, by turns curious, tender, indomitable. As readers, we are invited to dive deep into her unflinching observations, with the fierce confidence of the author herself, as would one asked to swim along with this well-conditioned swimmer, capable of 'penetrating the highest of high tides, swimming against every current, and testing the invisibility of the fishes.' The urge to stay with her, stroke by stroke, is a strong one; the portraits emerge, iconic as the boulder she spies at the edge of the shore in one of her poems, surfacing and resurfacing with the tide – an 'anchor and a strength' in a turbulent shoreline. There is a truth in these poems – at once unapproachable, mesmerizing, inescapable – to which we are all ultimately subject. And there is a reverence in these poems, tempered with both a longing to find passage across the distance between writer and subject and an acknowledgment of the forces keeping that from being possible. Ultimately, we are rewarded with an enduring sense of the inexpressible covalences of the heart, the eloquent push-pull of separation and connection, and the overwhelming fullness of our having experienced what is truly intimate in intimate relations."
–**George Wallace**, former writer-in-residence at the Walt Whitman Birthplace, poet laureate of Suffolk County, N.Y.

"John Berryman once told me that when he sent one of his last pre-publication manuscripts to Richard Wilbur, Wilbur replied kindly but said that John's poems could use more 'voltage.' Reading J.C. Hand's poetry, I keep thinking that she has the requisite voltage, the electrical gists and piths that keep my eye and mind moving with her voice down the page in jolts of strobe light. Consider a poem, in *East of July* (2004), each of whose five sections begins 'You raped me in Dubrovnik.' I've it read many times and have felt I've needed a surge-protector. Over the decades, after believing she has not belonged to herself, she has sometimes been defiled, but she has been determined not to be diminished into one of those 'lady writers / active in the garden club / used to rhyming posies / with rosies / penning light verse / into spiral notebooks.' With a kind of ferocious need, she has moved psychically from the home she felt to be her husband's only to a house (or houses) that in fact and in poetry are now hers

and to restore her to herself in time (the quotidian) and Time (spiritual eternity or at least depths within present being). In this new and riveting collection, *Mommy*, the places of her life and family are restored for her and her reader within 'a reverent kind of distance' ('A Summer Offering'). By way of both her interfused themes and the intensity of her saying, J.C. Hand is a sometimes shocking, often consoling, but always memorable poet. Emily Dickinson and Anne Sexton welcome her into their sisterhood."
–**William Heyen**, Ph.D., professor of English/poet-in-residence emeritus at The College at Brockport, SUNY

"What strikes me is the way (J.C. Hand) has made the words just flow so smoothly. It really is masterful. ... I can just picture (her) dancing and (her) imaginary leaps into the heights, even the sky."
–**Rabbi Adam D. Fisher**, Long Island poet

PAST PRAISE FOR JOAN CAROLE HAND

J.C. Hand's "writing teems with life, life in motion, life in color, life in sound, in sense, in sensuous ironic passion. Her work lives on. The reader lives with it."
–**Elliott Coleman**, founder Johns Hopkins University Writing Seminars

"J.C. Hand's writing is exciting to follow. One wants to discover where it is going and why, and the reader stays alert, feeling so much more aware of objects and events. She writes sensuously, deep into the flesh, very much herself."
–**David Ignatow**, poet, winner of the Bollingen Prize, editor of *American Poetry Review, Analytic, Beloit Poetry Journal*, and poetry editor of *The Nation*

"It is a poetry of confrontation, lyrical only in its anguish that is absolved, finally, by an undomesticated wit and intelligence."
–**Allen Planz**, former poet-in-residence at the Walt Whitman Birthplace, National Endowment for the Arts fellow, Pushcart Prize winner

"What I sense happening is an important thing, a process rarely attended, more rarely caught as clearly as J.C. Hand does it … From the tedium of ordinary, what Coleridge calls 'the lethargy of custom,' cities, suburbs, too many houses, there subtly and snakily emerges a feeling of myth … The redpoint of desire moves, furtive and insecure, and the characters follow to the empty times before dawn. The myth summons its dancers; sadly too, it lets them go. Between arsis and thesis, upbeat and the footstep final of the depleted dancer, the author attends minutely the passage through a detailed world."
–**Robert Kelly**, Asher B. Edelman Professor of Literature, Bard College, past poet laureate of Dutchess County, N.Y.

"I know the genuine article when I am hit by it!"
–**Edward Butscher**, poet, novelist, author of *Sylvia Plath: Method and Madness*

"J.C. Hand writes so efficiently, every word is important. … The writing is full and promising as pregnancy – building up to beautiful characters, complete and human."
–**Tere Ríos**, author, *The Fifteenth Pelican*, basis of the *Flying Nun*

"*Entrances to Nowhere* is a soaring experience into the inner soul."
–**Nikki Giovanni**, poet, author, *New York Times* best-seller, seven-time NAACP Image Awards winner

www.ingramcontent.com/pod-product-compliance
Lightning Source LLC
Chambersburg PA
CBHW031220090426
42740CB00009B/1250